# So, You're In Charge of
# Fundraising

**Fundraising tips, ideas, checklists, sample letters and more to help you raise money and awareness for your group or organization.**

## Dee Spruce

**iUniverse, Inc.**
New York   Bloomington

## So, You're in Charge of Fundraising!

Fundraising tips, ideas, checklists, sample
letters and more to help you raise money and
awareness for your group or organization.

*Copyright © 2010 by Dee Spruce*

*iUniverse books may be ordered through booksellers or by contacting:*

*iUniverse
1663 Liberty Drive
Bloomington, IN 47403
www.iuniverse.com
1-800-Authors (1-800-288-4677)*

*ISBN: 978-1-4502-7018-2 (pbk)
ISBN: 978-1-4502-7019-9 (ebk)*

*Printed in the United States of America
iUniverse rev. date: 11/12/10*

## Dedicated to…

Scott, my best friend, my husband. The years are flying by, but, as you often say, it has been a wonderful experience. I look forward to all that God has planned for us on the rest of our journey. Thank you for loving me unconditionally and supporting my every effort! I love you more today than ever and I'm so blessed to be your wife!

Tyler, my oldest daughter. It's hard to believe that you are all grown up and out in the world pursuing your dreams. I love you with all my heart and I am so proud of the incredible young woman you have become. Continue to focus on the prize baby girl! Seek God first and everything else will fall into place. I promise!

Colbi, my middle daughter. Your smile lights up my heart. Who knew you'd grow up so fast? Just yesterday it seems you were playing on the swing set in the backyard and now you're a sophomore in college! You've become quite the young lady and I couldn't be more proud of who you are today. I love you bunches!

Tanner, my son. Well, Tannerman, it's hard to believe you just got your learner's permit and you're driving. You are such an amazing young man and you have so many unique qualities that will surely take you far in life, especially that sense of humor of yours. I know God has great plans for you, trust in Him always son and know that I love you dearly and I always will!

Friends and family who have encouraged and prayed for me along the way. Thank you for believing in me!

And to God, I am so thankful for your grace, mercy, and many blessings!

# Introduction

"You do not have because you do not ask" (James 4:2). This has been a phrase I have used over and over again for years. I have used it on board members who "didn't feel comfortable" asking people for money. I have used it on non-profit directors who were afraid of hearing the big "No!" I've used it on people who wanted me to raise money for their groups and organizations. I've even used it while asking potential donors for gifts.

After 20 years of working with non-profits, I decided to put what I've learned down on paper. Within the pages of this book I am offering, to each of you, my knowledge and experience as a *beggar*! Okay, not really, what I meant to say was, as a *fundraiser.*

When I walk into a business people usually raise their eyebrows and, before I even walk in the door, I hear "How much do you want and when do you need it?" We all have gifts and most people will tell you that mine is raising money. I have to say, I think I am pretty good at it. It takes a certain knack, a salesman's mentality, combined with the gift of gab, the ability to handle rejection (on occasion), a strong belief in the cause, and ultimately God's grace!

If you are afraid to ask you are in the wrong business! Fundraising is after all by definition: the process of soliciting and gathering money or other gifts in kind, by "key word" *requesting* donations from individuals, businesses, charitable foundations, or governmental agencies. So, if you are in charge of your organization's fundraising, it's time to get used to asking!

These next chapters will provide you with ideas and suggestions for successful fundraising events. All you have to do is choose those that are right for you and your group. I've laid each one out from start to finish, so have at it! Included are also sample letters, flyers, and checklists. While most of my samples are specific to events held through the Crisis Pregnancy Center please tweak them to meet your organization's needs.

Whether you are looking for simple fundraisers to help your Scout Troop or you're ready to put on that huge banquet to raise half of your organization's budget, this is the book for you! Grab a highlighter and a glass of sweet tea (yep, Carolina girl!) and let's get you headed in the right direction!

# FUNDRAISING
# BANQUETS/DINNERS

My favorite event every year as the Director of a local Crisis Pregnancy Center has been our Annual Fundraising Banquet. This event is key to raising the funds needed to carry on the work of the Center. The goal for the event is to, not only raise funds, but also to solicit one-time and monthly pledges throughout the year.

While I tend to work best under pressure and tight time constraints, the general rule for a smoothly planned banquet is to start working on it six months in advance. The reason I say this is because if you are considering a National Speaker, which I highly recommend, you are going to want to make sure you can get them before their calendar is booked for the year.

In the initial planning of your event, you will need to start thinking about whom you'd like to ask to be on your Banquet Committee. Please make sure this is

*Dee Spruce*

a committee of peers who have a true heart for your cause and who are not afraid to, you guessed it, "ask!" I put together my budget, choose my date and the venue, then spend some time researching speakers. I then obtain board approval of my plan before pulling the committee together to work on the logistics and marketing of the event.

Your event budget should include projected income and expenses. If this is your first banquet you will need to do a bit of dreaming in this department, unless of course you already wrote specifics into your regular budget for the event. If you have held banquets in the past, use your income and expense reports to project for this event, of course while increasing your anticipated income this year! Income should include: underwriting, ticket sales, love offering, monthly pledges and one-time pledges. Expenses should include: speaker (honorarium, travel, and accommodations), venue, meals, printing, advertising and decorations.

Once you have determined your budget for the event, pick your date and venue. A sample Banquet Checklist is available at the end of this chapter. Keep in mind that the best nights of the week to hold fundraising banquets are on Tuesdays or Thursdays. Mondays tend to be meeting nights, Wednesdays are church nights, and weekends are for rest and family. That's not to say that a Friday or Saturday night event wouldn't be successful, however; it

4

has been my experience that people are more available on Tuesdays or Thursdays.

Your venue should be a central location to your organization and your service area. Make sure the facility you are using has adequate parking and will allow you to post any required signage outside your event. You will need to make sure you have well maintained bathroom facilities and that a kitchen will be available if you are using an off-sight caterer. It is helpful if you find a location that already has tables and chairs available; then you won't have the added expense of rentals. Before signing your contract, make sure you are clear on what their staff will do to assist with your event from set-up to clean-up. I also always request the opportunity to set up and decorate the night before. I then just add finishing touches, like balloons or flowers, on the day of the event. I have never been charged extra to set up the night before, of course I've never been afraid to ask either!

While there are several booking agencies and speakers bureaus that can assist you with choosing the right person for your event, I would highly recommend using Single Source Speakers. I have worked with Ron Miller and his staff for years and have never been disappointed! You can view their roster of speakers at www.singlesourcespeakers. com. The SSS staff is very knowledgeable of their speakers and they are sure to offer up a perfect match for your event.

The right speaker will make your event a huge success! The wrong speaker will reflect in your donations without a doubt. I know this from real experience, trust me; choose wisely! Also, realize that great speakers may come with large honorariums. I once had a speaker that charged $15,000. Guess what, I paid $7,500! Don't be afraid to "ask" if the speaker might negotiate his or her honorarium. I can think of numerous times when I wrote a letter to the speaker through the speakers bureau to request a discount on an honorarium; only once was I denied that request. Don't forget that you will need to take care of travel, meals, and accommodations for your speaker. Most agencies require a deposit up front at the signing of the contract. You can seek out someone to specifically underwrite this expense or just pull from your general budget with the understanding that, once it starts coming in, underwriting will accommodate for that deduction.

Very rarely have I used a speaker that was close enough to my organization to drive. If that is something your speaker can do, plan to compensate them the IRS mileage rate for their trip. For those that fly, I don't ever pay for first class tickets. In fact, I once had a speaker who would only fly first class; I pulled my request and sent a letter of disappointment! People who are being hired to help raise funds for non-profit charities and ministries need to have a heart for those organizations. Flying coach to the event should not be seen as something that is beneath them.

Most of the speakers I have worked with over the years prefer to be picked up at the airport rather than driving themselves. A taxi to the hotel is fine, if you are in close proximity. I recommend asking a board member or volunteer to pick up the speaker at the airport and help them get settled in. I also have this same individual drive them to the event. This gives your board member an opportunity to share with your speaker their heart for your organization.

Accommodations for speakers really depend on their personal preferences. I have had speakers that felt very comfortable staying in the guest room at my house or the home of one of our board members or volunteers. This is a lot to ask; having them at my home made for some extra hustling and bustling for me. Hotels are your best bet! We also have some incredible bed and breakfasts in our town that I have utilized. When making arrangements for a place to stay, keep in mind the needs of your speaker: meals, gym, internet access, handicap access, etc. Most speakers fly in on the day of the event and leave that same evening or sometimes the next morning, so it shouldn't be that difficult to find adequate accommodations for one night.

On that same note, I have never paid for my speaker to stay at a hotel or bed and breakfast, you shouldn't either. Visit the owner or manager and explain who you are and what you are doing. For some, it will be such an honor to have your "nationally known" speaker stay at their business they won't even charge! For others, you might consider offering to include them in your program as an underwriter or sponsor for your event. It may require a request in writing, but it will be worth it in the end!

Okay, so you have your date, your venue, and you have signed the contract with your speaker. Now it's on to determining the theme of your event. It is very important to have your theme appeal to the audience you are inviting! For ministries it may be a scripture verse, for some it may be centered on your organization's anniversary or you might want to make your theme reflective of your speaker's testimony. Once you have that narrowed down, you need to start considering how you will decorate for the event. These are all initial duties that can be accomplished by the director of the organization or by the committee. As mentioned before, I like to do the preliminary work and then organize with my committee.

So, it's been nearly three months since you started on this, three more months to go before the event! Time to start working with your committee to secure any special musicians, a sound man, and equipment you may need, PA system, overhead, etc.

Let me give you some great advice while considering musicians, "This is not about displaying local talent, it's about raising money!" Everything that you do at this event needs to be done for the purpose of bringing in money for your organization. For many years we tied in musicians and an auction to our banquets. After much research, I tried for several years to minimize the events at my banquets. Not only was it less hassle, it was more successful financially. I would suggest a guest emcee, but, other than that, let this night be about your Guest Speaker and whoever is doing your financial appeal.

This is also the time for you to designate specific tasks to your committee. I would suggest actually assigning tasks to one or two members on your committee and give them the authority to form a subcommittee to complete these tasks. You will need someone handling finances, including ticket sales and sponsorships, public relations and marketing, set-up (unless the venue staff does this), decorations, greeting and seating, and everyone's favorite….clean-up!

Your Finance Committee will be responsible for underwriting or sponsorships and ticket sales. I have found it best to utilize table hosts for ticket sales at banquets. Some organizations choose instead to find corporate sponsorships for tables and to give tickets away for free. You may have to speak with other organizations in your area to see what works best for you. It's nice to have an established list of individuals or companies on file to approach for underwriting and sponsorship. Create a letter highlighting your event and the anticipated results, for example: community awareness, increase volunteers, fund a specific project, or keep the doors open! Include your goal in the request for underwriting and sponsorship. If receiving $5,000 would help you completely underwrite the cost of the event, allowing every dollar raised that evening to be used directly for your goal, then put that in the letter! Also, add the "what's in it for you," whether it be a signage at the event or a mention in all promotions. Mail the letter and follow-up within one week with a phone call or visit. You know your donors, if a face to face would be more effective, then schedule one!

If you choose to go with underwriting of expenses and ticket sales, establish a list of couples who have a true heart for your organization to serve as table hosts for your event. Determine how many tables your venue can hold and plan for a couple hosts per table. Utilize your church contacts to build this list, as well as your regular donors. Each board member, staff member, and volunteer should also be utilized as a table host. It is very important to explain to your table hosts what their role will be at the event. If you set up tables of eight, you will want to give your "host couple" their tickets and six to sell. Usually our hosts will also pay for their tickets, but offering them free as a "thank you" would be nice, as well. Provide a packet with a letter thanking them for taking on this role and with specific instructions on what you want accomplished. I have provided a sample host letter and instruction sheet. I also put the host's name on their set of tickets, so we can easily direct attendees to their appropriate table.

You may want to allow for one or two tables in your organization's name for those that call who are not connected to a table host. Call-ins can be placed on a list and plugged in to available seats at host's tables or your organization's table. It is vital that you fill seats! If you can combine tables in the end, do so and eliminate those you set aside in your name. The goal is a packed and sold out event!

Make sure your hosts understand that this is a fundraising event and they should make sure that those they invite expect "the ask." Also, express that it is an adult only event. The great thing about utilizing table hosts is that you have the opportunity to have those who truly support your ministry invite people in "their circles" whom you may not have otherwise been able to reach! They are also able to hold their invited guests accountable to attend the event. Host packets should be distributed four to six weeks in advance, with a deadline of one week prior to the event, in order to collect monies and any tickets that aren't sold. Once you've collected that information, you can begin to plug in people who have called for tickets, as a result of your promotion, and utilize the tables that have seats available.

Your Public Relations and Marketing committee should create a list with contact information for all local radio stations, cable outlets, and newspapers. Either you need to create a Press Release or ask them to do so in order to get your announcements out to the public. If finances permit, you can purchase ad space from a media source, however; I have always had great success utilizing the Community Awareness section or the What's Happening section of my newspapers. The local cable companies and radio stations will run your announcements at no charge, as well! Be sure to place the event information on your website and utilize sites like facebook, twitter, or any blogs you participate in for free event promotion!

Your Set-up Committee should plan to be at the venue the day before to work with you on getting any signage up and putting your floor plan together. Their work is going to be right before your event. This committee should also plan on helping with the set-up of any sound equipment or props for your stage, such as a podium or projector screen.

Your Decorations Committee should work with you to secure all the items needed for decorating your venue. I personally love to decorate, it is a form of stress relief for me. Remember that you should already have a vision in mind. Share this vision with the committee and brainstorm ideas that you all agree upon. Then, begin collecting the pieces you will need for the event. I suggest that you avoid using balloons on the tables; they tend to get in the way when people are looking at the stage. If you do decide to use them, remind guests to put them on the floor prior to your program starting. Don't forget to label your table with a sign that has your table host's last name on it. That will make seating a great deal easier!

I have used some unusual antics to come up with decorations over the years! My craziest inspiration came from a throw pillow I saw at Wal-Mart! I usually go to stores before events and browse through furnishings and home décor until something jumps out at me for a theme. That year the pillow I found was black, orangey-red, gray, and white with a tropical pattern. Once you determine your theme, color, logo, and decorations you should plan on using those throughout your marketing pieces. I used white invitations with black print. The tables had white table cloths with black votive candles scattered throughout. The votive holders were placed on small round mirrored tiles (over the years I have collected glassware from yard sales and estate sales). I then took different sized goblets and crystal glasses and placed them scattered between the votives. Some of the goblets were overflowing with silver ribbon, while others had one goldfish swimming inside. I also wrapped black napkins and silverware with red ribbon and placed those at each place setting. Our program for the evening was printed in silver and gray. For the stage, I borrowed plants from our local nursery and adorned them with white lights. The bottom of the stage was draped with white tulle and lights.

I received many compliments that year for our event. In fact, one attendee asked to borrow the goblets for her son's rehearsal dinner. I found out she too used goldfish for her decorations.

I learned many years ago that flea markets were some of my favorite places to shop for decorating pieces for my events. Over the years, I have collected goblets, vases, mirrored tiles, candle holders, silk flowers, and all kinds of items that I utilize year after year. I always try to make purchases that I can use again at a future event.

It would be nice if you could provide a small token to give each guest as a special gift. At one banquet our theme was "Dining with the Stars." Each place setting had a silver star ornament for guests to take as a gift. The stars also served as table decorations. The stage area of your event will be a focal point, so make sure you remember this in your decorating plan. Local florists will often allow you to borrow plants to use on stage for free if you agree to include them in your program and promotions as an event sponsor. If you work with children or families, perhaps you could have a few posters made of your clients and place them on art easels on stage. Easels can be borrowed from your local arts council, art gallery, or school art program at no charge. Remember when decorating that less is more!

Your Greeting and Seating Committee should consist of your organization's Director, several members of the Board of Directors, and your Bookkeeper or Office Manager. The Director should plan to spend as much time as possible greeting guests as they arrive. This one-on-one contact is very important at charitable events. Board members should be positioned at key places in the room to help guests find their seats; each one should have a copy of your seating chart for the evening. Your Bookkeeper or Office Manager should be available for guests who need to drop off ticket money to help keep things flowing; have him or her seated near the door, but not in an area that blocks the flow of traffic.

Your Clean-up Committee is responsible for breaking down after your event. Make sure they pick up any programs, pledge cards and envelopes, and decorations that are left on the table for possible re-use. We often utilize our local youth programs for this part of the event, with a few adult supervisors. Make sure you have clear instructions printed out for them prior to the event. Also, make sure you establish ground rules with regards to what they need to wear, cell phone use, and whether or not they should eat prior to the event.

Print material for the event should be designed through your Event Committee. This will include: flyers, posters, tickets, and programs. Your program should provide an overview of your organization with a brief description of programs and services, as well as year-to-date statistics. It is nice to also include the names of your board, staff and any underwriters or event sponsors. There should also be a simple schedule for the evening.

Remember to stay focused on the purpose of your event. Stick to your agenda and stay on a strict timeline! I would suggest you allot half an hour for seating, a few minutes for greeting, an opening prayer and blessing, then move right into your meal. My events usually run from 6:30pm to 9:00pm. Big rule of thumb is to make sure your plea is presented before 9:00pm! For every minute after that, I've seen people get up and leave and money walk right out the door! After all of your guests have been served and the majority are finished eating, move on with the program! Also, please make sure that anyone who speaks at the event, emcee or pastor, does not make a financial plea. That should be left up to whomever is doing your appeal and done at the proper time in your program. You should give anyone working on the program specific instructions on what you need and what not to do at the event.

Who should do your appeal and how? Well, this one is really up to you! Some speakers request that you allow them to fulfill this duty. That should be determined up-front. If you choose to let your speaker or perhaps a prominent supporter do your appeal, please, please, please make sure you work with them in advance and know exactly what they will say and do. Over the years I have experimented with several different approaches to the appeal. I have to tell you that the Two Part Appeal that is taught by David Bereit has been the most successful for our organization. Visit his website and get the training, it works! http://increaseyourbanquetincome.com/.

I have included samples of One and Two Part Appeal cards for your convenience. If you are working with table hosts, I suggest preparing an envelope for each table with the plea cards and envelopes in them. Then, distribute those to your hosts and ask that they hold them until they are asked to distribute the materials to their guests. If you don't have hosts, you can either have your youth servers pass the cards out or have them available at each table setting. Don't forget to provide pens too! I have found that if the cards are provided prior to the appeal, some people will fill them out at the beginning of the event and be done. That's not what you want! The preconceived thoughts of what they will commit to donate will go on your pledge card without any knowledge of who you are, what you have, and what you hope to accomplish. Your speaker and appeal process, along with prayer, prayer, prayer, will open their hearts to give as the Lord guides! We all know this entire event is about appealing to hearts and checkbooks....that's why it's a fundraiser, right?

Client testimonies are great additions to your program. I suggest that you either consider a client or two to testify at the event or have a DVD or PowerPoint created that shows your organization and client interactions. By doing the latter, you can have some control over what is said; not that a client would say something wrong, intentionally anyways. If you choose a client testimony, I suggest that you have him or her write out what will be said and review it before the event. Also, be sure to assign a staff member to stand on stage with the client for support.

I prefer the DVD. You know the saying, "A picture is worth a thousand words!" Pictures of your staff, volunteers, clients and programs set to a song that parallels your mission will be priceless. I have used our local university's Media Department students, home school students, and a local company to make DVD's over the years. Cost has been minimal.

The testimony or DVD should be done either before your One Part Appeal or in the middle of your Two Part Appeal. Once your appeal is done, instruct attendees to pass their cards to their table hosts and then have them collected at that time by your youth servers.

Make sure that you have a staff member or board member positioned at the doorways while attendees are exiting to thank them for attending your event. This is also a great opportunity to get feedback on their thoughts on the evening!

It's important to follow-up with a thank you letter to everyone who donated, prior to your event and within a week after the event. Be sure to share your success in the letter, as well. Also, send out a confirmation of pledges with a self-addressed envelope for their convenience to every attendee that made a pledge to your organization.

## Banquet Underwriting Letter

Dear Supporter of Life,

It is with great excitement that I am writing you this letter! It is so hard to believe that we are in the midst of the 20th year of service to the unborn and families here in northeastern North Carolina. So many lives have been affected by our work and we realize that it is all made possible by the generous support of people like you!

We are already in the midst of planning our Annual Fundraising Banquet on April 7th at Nixon's Catering in Edenton. This year's Guest Speaker is Henry Jernigan. Henry is from Burlington, NC and we are honored to have him be a part of this event. Henry and his wife found out they were expecting after one year of marriage. Doctors told them that the baby had Spina Bifida and would most likely never walk. It was recommended that they consider terminating the pregnancy. Henry and his wife decided to trust God with their baby and stood fast in their faith choosing life for son, Pierce! This family's testimony promises to bring laughter and tears, as Henry shares their son's journey.

As always, to put on our banquet we need the help from supporters like you. Please consider a donation to help us underwrite the cost of this year's event. Your gift will allow us to cover our up-front expenses so that we do not have to pull funds out of the Center's operating budget. Our goal is to cover all expenses so that every penny made during the event can go straight to the work of the Crisis Pregnancy Center.

Your prayerful consideration is greatly appreciated. We thank God for your continued faithfulness to this ministry. May He bless you today and forever!

Gratefully!

## Banquet Ticket Host Packet Letter

Dear Ticket Host/Hostess,

Thank you so much for your willingness to host a table of eight for our Annual Fundraising Banquet on Tuesday, April 17th. We guarantee you and your guests an unforgettable evening of fellowship, excitement, and, of course, challenge! This year's speaker is known worldwide for his stance on "Life," brother of Terry Schiavo, Bobby Schindler. We have included a copy of his bio with this letter for your information.

As you consider those you will be inviting to this event, please prayerfully consider whom the Lord would have participate. Who do you know is a person of influence? A person who may be willing to give of their time, talents, or treasures? Special friends of the center help to underwrite portions of this event. In order for us to be good stewards of God's money, we must let people know that this is a FUNDRAISING dinner for the ACPC and there will be a plea for financial support and pledges of time and talent. The sacrificial giving of the sponsors is intended to increase the giving of those attending the banquet, therefore; we must request that only adults attend

The purpose of this event is to introduce new people to the ministry and to share the eternal impact we are making in the Albemarle area. This event produces new volunteers, donors, and clients, all of which are vital to this ministry.

Enclosed you will find your guest list, instructions, and eight tickets. Please return your ticket money and guest list to the center by Thursday, April 12th. Also, please take a few minutes to carefully read over the enclosed instructions before you begin inviting your guests. If you have any questions please call the Center @ xxx-xxxx.

Thank you for being ambassadors for our Center! You will make a difference by inviting your friends and acquaintances. We are grateful for your investment!

In His Service,

## Banquet Ticket Host Information and Instructions

1.  Personally invite your guests and make sure they know the date, time, place, etc. There will be a charge of $25.00 per person this year. Please give tickets to your guests only when the money is received.

2.  Make sure guests understand that this is a special evening with Henry Jernigan, but that it is also a fundraiser. A plea for support will be given at the event. This is an **adult-only** event.

3.  We need you to sell all of your tickets to your church/organization. However, our purpose is not to just get the tickets sold. We need this event's attendees to help us raise the funds necessary to keep our doors open. Please keep that in mind when choosing your guests.

4.  Please return your ticket money to the center by April 2nd (envelope enclosed). <u>We must have this information returned on time in order to remain our schedule.</u>

5.  Dress for the event is "church/business" attire.

6.  Please plan to arrive 15 minutes early so that you can greet your table guests as they arrive at the event; unless you want to bid at the silent auction! Then, arrive at 6:00pm ☺!

7.  Call and remind your guests two or three days before the event of the time and location.

Pray! Pray! Pray! He will show you whom to invite. Sometimes the person you expect least is the person God has prepared to give above and beyond all we could ask or imagine (physically, financially, and prayerfully)!

Thank you so much for your support! If you have any questions, please call the center at xxx-xxxx.

### Banquet Invitation

Table Host _____

**Albemarle Crisis Pregnancy Center**

Annual Fundraising Banquet
Tuesday, April 13th
American Legion Bldg, Chowan Fairgrounds.
Edenton
6:00 p.m. Seating
6:30 p.m. Dinner and Program
Ticket Price: $20.00
Menu: Chicken breast, Roast Beef, mashed potatoes, green beans, rolls, tea and dessert

Former Planned Parenthood Director Abby Johnson, 29, quit her job after experiencing a "change of heart" while participating in an abortion procedure at her Texas clinic. Abby has now joined the group Coalition for Life which prays regularly outside the clinic where she worked.

*All proceeds benefit the*
*Albemarle Crisis Pregnancy Center*

Encouraging teens, enhancing families, empowering women... all for life!

**Banquet**

**One-Time Pledge Card**

## YES! HERE IS MY MOST GENEROUS ONE-TIME GIFT TO HELP END ABORTION AND STRENGTHEN FAMILIES IN NORTHEASTERN NORTH CAROLINA

MY ONE-TIME GIFT: [ ] $5,000  [ ]$2,500  [ ]$1,000  [ ]$500  [ ]$250  [ ]$100 []
OTHER:_____

NAME_____     [ ] I HAVE ENCLOSED CASH OR A
        CHECK FOR MY ONE GIFT

ADDRESS_____     [ ] CHARGE MY CREDIT CARD FOR MY
        ONE-TIME GIFT:

CITY/STATE/ZIP_____CARD
        NUMBER_____

PHONE_____     [ ] VISA [ ] MASTERCARD EXP.
        DATE_____

EMAIL_____
        SIGNATURE_____

ALBEMARLE CRISIS PREGNANCY CENTER 123 MAIN STREET CITY, NC 27906 xxx-xxx-xxxx. EMAIL:ACPCEC@EMBARQMAIL.COM

**Banquet**

**Monthly Pledge Card**

# YES! OVER THE NEXT 12 MONTHS YOU CAN COUNT ON ME TO HELP THE

## ALBEMARLE CRISIS PREGNANCY CENTER CHANGE HEARTS AND SAVE LIVES!

MY PLEDGE: [ ] $500 [ ] $250 [ ] $100 [ ] $50 [ ] $30 [ ] OTHER: _____

CHECK ONE: [ ] MONTHLY [ ] QUARTERLY [ ] ANNUALLY (PLEDGE BEGINS IN MAY)

NAME_____ [ ] PLEASE SEND ME A MONTHLY STATEMENT AND I

WILL MAIL IN MY PLEDGE

ADDRESS_____ [ ] CHARGE MY CREDIT CARD FOR MY PLEDGE:

CITY/STATE/ZIP_____ CARD

NUMBER_____

PHONE_____ [ ] VISA [ ] MASTERCARD EXP.DATE____/____

EMAIL_____

SIGNATURE_____

ALBEMARLE CRISIS PREGNANCY CENTER 123 MAIN STREET CITY, NC 27906 xxx-xxx-xxxx. EMAIL.ACPCPC@ EMBARQMAIL.COM

## Banquet Pledge Letter

Dear Supporter of Life!

Thank you so much for being a part of our 2010 Annual Fundraising Banquet. You are such a valuable part of this ministry and all that we have accomplished over the years.

I trust that our speaker, Abby Johnson, was a blessing to you, as she was to me! I'm so excited that God has moved in her life and she is now uniting with those of us in the pro-life movement sharing the truth about Planned Parenthood!

Remember, if we each seize every opportunity to make our voices heard regarding issues pertaining to Life; together we can dispel the myth that we are the silent minority and expose the lies of Satan!

Thank you for being a part of our efforts and for your generous banquet pledge of _____! We have enclosed 12 self-addressed envelopes for your convenience.

If you are interested in being added to our mailing list so that you can receive updates on issues regarding our ministry please send us your email address to acpcec@ embarqmail.com.

Together we can!

Blessings,

Dee Spruce

Executive Director,

Albemarle Crisis Pregnancy Centers


**Banquet Checklist:**

1.  Six Months Prior:
___Choose banquet date and venue

___Secure location via deposit and contract

___Choose Speaker and secure with deposit and contract

___Choose banquet theme

___Secure Caterer via contract

___Banquet proposal to board with contracts for final approval

2.  Three Months Prior:
___Choose special musicians and secure for event

___Artwork creation for invitations and posters

___Secure PA system and operator

___Order items for special gifts for guests

___Organize Committees for: PR, set-up, decorating, greeting/seating, clean-up

3.  Two Months Prior:

___Send underwriting letters

___Contact table hosts

___Secure accommodations for Speaker

___Order posters and invitations

___Secure emcee, pastors for opening and closing prayer, person to do plea

4.  Six Weeks Prior:

___Send out table host packets, tickets, and invitations

___Mail letters to pastors

___Speaker bio to local press for prior event promotion and event coverage

___Get Public Service Announcements to local radio stations, television and   newspapers

___Line up servers for event

___Design program and pledge cards and send to printer

___Do agenda for event

5.  Four Weeks Prior:

___Focus on decorations for event, purchase or gather needed items

___Secure table linens, purchase needed tableware

___Visit venue to brainstorm and set-up ideas for event

___Create diagram of table set-up (this will help greeters guide guests to their   tables)

___Contact table hosts for follow-up

___Choose client for testimony

6.  One Week Prior:
___Collect all ticket money

___Create table signs with host information

___Follow-up with all participants and committee members

___Print registration sheets for tables

___Send a copy of your "Policy on Speaking" on behalf of the agency, plea cards   and agenda to emcee and plea giver

___Pack up items for event

# FOOD SALES

## Plate Sales

PTA, FFA, 4-H, Cub Scouts, Youth Groups and even CPC's hold Annual Plate sales as fundraisers. This is a no-brainer way to bring in some quick income for any charity or ministry. Combine this with an auction, bake sale, craft show, or yard sale and you can get even more change for your efforts!

As always determine the goal for your event. What do you want to raise and what will you do with it? Choose a date, decide on lunch and supper (or one or the other), book a pick-up point, then contact a local caterer. In our area, chicken and barbecue plates are a big seller. Your area, however, might do better with a different menu. Our caterers provide the food, plates, and plastic ware. We provide the labor to put the plates together and get them out the door!

When choosing your menu, remember to think about the weather. You don't want potato salad or coleslaw sitting around waiting to be picked up in 98 degree weather! You also don't want your warm fried chicken iced cold because it's 5 below! We generally go for a meat, green veggie, and a starch, then throw in a roll and dessert bar. Spaghetti dinners have also been big sellers.

Simply visit a local printer or check with your caterer to see if they provide tickets. Set a goal of how many plates you want to sell. We've done events in this area that sold 2,500 to 5,000 plates. Aim high! When choosing your price, be sure to consider what you're paying for the plates. When approaching the caterer remind them it's a fundraiser and try to negotiate your cost. In general, we pay around $3.95 to $4.95 and price our tickets between $7.00 and $8.00.

Assign a good amount of tickets to every member of your organization and get the sales started approximately one month prior to the event. Solicit businesses, doctor's offices, hospitals, and schools in your area, especially if you are serving lunch. Many business owners will purchase tickets for their entire staff if you will provide delivery at lunch time.

Two weeks prior to the event, distribute Public Service Announcements to all of your local media channels. Line up shifts for those to prepare plates, run plates to cars, take tickets, and deliver meals. One week prior, talk with your caterer about the number of tickets sold so far. This number will increase slightly, as you will also have people who walk up to your event and purchase.

## Plate Sales Public Service Announcement

XYZ Youth Group Holds it's 2ⁿᵈ Annual Barbecue Fundraiser!

XYZ Youth Group will be holding it's Second Annual Barbecue Fundraiser on Saturday, March 29ᵗʰ from 11:00am to 2:00pm at the Wal-Mart parking lot in Elizabeth City. Tickets are $7.00 and include: barbecue, fried chicken, coleslaw, boiled potatoes, and a roll. Nixon Catering Company is providing the meal. All proceeds for this event will benefit XYZ Youth Group's summer mission trip to Pennsylvania. For tickets or further information call xxx.xxx.xxxx.

## Plate Sales Sample Ticket

*XYZ Youth Group*
Barbecue Fundraiser
When: Saturday, March 29th
Where: Wal-Mart Parking Lot, Elizabeth City
Time: 11:00am to 2:00pm
Ticket cost is $7.00
Nixon Family Restaurant Catering

## Plate Sales Checklist:

1. Three Months Prior:

___Form a committee to organize the event

___Determine a financial goal for the event

___Choose a date

___Determine your menu

___Secure a venue to hold your sale

___Contact local caterers

2. Two Months Prior:

___Secure a catering contact

___Get tickets printed

___Prepare flyers for advertising

3.  One Month Prior:

___Distribute tickets and start selling

___Distribute flyers within the community

___Prepare public service announcements

4.  Two Weeks Prior:

___Distribute public service announcements to all media channels

___Create event invitation and distribute on Facebook

___Set up team of servers, ticket takers, delivery people for event

5.  One Week Prior:

___Contact caterer with approximate number of tickets sold/anticipated sales

## Pizza Sales

Everybody loves pizza, or at least they should! As a recovering carbohydrate addict and cheese hog I can certainly attest to it! This is another one of those easy ways to bring some fast money into any size organization. Some people prefer this over a Plate Sale because there is no prep work, other than ticket sales.

Thursday or Friday evenings are great nights to hold this fundraiser. Who doesn't want to grab something on the way home from a long week of work to feed the family? Ticket sales will depend on what kind of deal you can get from your local pizzeria. Remember, it's a fundraiser. Decide what you're raising money for, decide how much you need, and send someone to the restaurant who isn't afraid to "ask" for a deal. Some places will deliver, but if your order is too large you may have to solicit some people to help with pick-up.

We have used one of the famous "chains" over the years and have been able to get a large, one topping for just $5. So, we price the tickets at $10 and make a pretty good return on our investment! Simply get tickets printed and distribute them to everyone in your organization for sale. A mere 500 pizzas sold and with the $5 deal, you can raise $2,500 in no time!

**Pizza Sales Flyer**

*It's time again! Support our band!*
Abba High School Band
Annual Pizza Sale Fundraiser
When: Friday, August 13, 2010
Where: Abba High School Cafeteria
Pick Up Times: 6:00pm to 8:00pm
AHB is now selling tickets for their annual pizza fundraiser. Please see any band

member to purchase tickets. Ticket cost is $10.00. Ticket is valid for one single topping pizza. Topping choices include: sausage, cheese, ham or pepperoni. All proceeds will be used to purchase new uniforms for our band next year!

*Goooooo………ABBA!*

## Pizza Sales Checklist:

1. Three Months Prior:
___Form a committee to organize the event

___Determine a financial goal for the event

___Choose a date

___Determine your pizza restaurant

___Secure a venue to hold your sale

2. Two Months Prior:
___Get tickets printed

___Prepare flyers advertising event

3. One Month Prior:
___Distribute tickets and start selling

___Distribute flyers in community

___Prepare public service announcements

4. Two Weeks Prior:
___Distribute public service announcements to all media channels

___Create event invitation and distribute on Facebook

___Set up team of people for event to pass out pizza and collect tickets/money

5.   One Week Prior:

___Contact restaurant with approximate number of tickets sold/anticipated sales

# BABY BOTTLE FUNDRAISER

## Baby Bottle Campaign

This fundraiser is one that we started several years ago after receiving information from a group called "Plans for You" promoting a Baby Bottle Boomerang. This event includes baby bottles that read God's Gift, which are distributed to supporters who, in turn, place loose change in them and return them to the Center when full. Check out their website for details www.plansforyou.org. This promotion has raised millions of dollars for pro life organizations across the country!

For years we had the same concept, but used homemade wooden baby blocks with our initials on them instead and placed them in churches and homes. The boxes were made and donated by one of our supporters who did wood working. Slots on the top of the block allowed people to drop in donations for the Center.

This was a great fundraiser and community awareness campaign, however; the blocks were big and bulky and, in all honesty, in need of painting or replacement. So, we decided to make it more efficient and switch to the baby bottle concept!

In order to make this fundraiser more personal to our Center we decided to solicit donations of baby bottles from local businesses and organizations. On each bottle we put a tag that had the first name and birth date (no last names and no year for confidentiality) of one of our babies. These were then distributed to churches, youth groups, women's ministries, and individuals. The object is to have people pray for the baby whose name is on their bottle each day and to put their loose change or dollar bills in the bottle to help raise funds for the Center. This is a win-win situation; the center raises much needed funds, and prayers are going up on a daily basis for our little ones!

We try to promote this during Sanctity of Human Life in January of each year, but have some groups that like to do this as an ongoing effort to support our Center. Anytime we speak on behalf of the Center we take bottles with us! People have fun choosing a boy, a girl, or a child with a birth date that is symbolic to them because of an anniversary or birthday of their own.

We have raised tens of thousands of dollars through this campaign! It is low cost and requires little effort by staff, unless you don't have access to a change counting machine! Then, it requires a lot of change counting and rolling by volunteers and staff alike!

## Baby Bottle Campaign Flyer
## Baby Bottle What?

The CPC will be holding an ongoing Baby Bottle Campaign throughout this year. If your church or business is looking for a tangible way to get involved with our work at the Crisis Pregnancy Center, here it is!

Baby bottles will be picked up at the Center or delivered to a church or business contact any time during 2009. Bottles may be distributed to individuals, groups (Sunday School classes, Youth Groups, GA's, etc.) or to families. Each bottle is labeled with the name of a baby that was born to one of our center clients.

We ask that you pray for the baby on your bottle, as well as that baby's parents. Then, just place your loose change in the bottle each day until it is full and return it to the Center or to your church or business contact. We would also ask that you prayerfully consider any size of currency; checks may be put in the bottles, as well.

We have much to do at the CPC in 2009 and we are trusting that the BBC will get us off to a good start! Thank you for your willingness to participate in this project. Your involvement allows us to continue our mission of sharing truth in love to women and families in the Albemarle area.

For questions or concerns please feel free to call our office at xxx-xxxx or you can email the Center at www.centeremail.com.

## Baby Bottle Campaign Checklist:

1.  Three Months Prior:
    ___Form a committee to organize campaign

    ___Determine financial goal

    ___Choose time-frame for campaign

    ___Determine distribution channels for bottles

    ___Begin soliciting for and collecting baby bottles

2.  Two Months Prior:
    ___Create list of contacts for churches, civic groups, etc. that will participate

    ___Create a letter explaining campaign and campaign goals

    ___Create flyers to be sent out with letter

    ___Call contacts to confirm commitment to participate

___Determine how distribution of bottles will take place

3.  One Month Prior:
___Print labels for bottles

___Laminate labels

___Put labels on bottles

___Mail letters and flyers to committed contacts

___Prepare directions sheet to be distributed with bottles

4.  Two Weeks Prior:
___Contact participants to determine number of bottles needed

___Sort bottles for each group

___Bag bottles with directions and extra flyer

5.  One Week Prior:
___Distribute bottles to groups

# TEN FOR TEN CAMPAIGN

Our organization started doing this campaign last year while looking for an opportunity to solicit support from our immediate area. We thought of the idea and created the campaign based on similarities to the March of Dimes and Cancer Society campaigns.

It's really rather simple! Our board and staff (the 10 of us) each came to the table with the names of 10 friends or family members we felt would help with the campaign. Each of those 100 were given packets with 10 letters, 10 envelopes for mailing, and 10 return envelopes for donations to the Center.

The idea is to get those 100 individuals to send out letters to 10 friends and family members asking them for a one-time donation of $10 to help support our ministry. Usually, friends and family support the causes that their loved ones support! So, with a carefully written letter and all the needed mailing supplies, we filled in names and addressed envelopes for those who agreed to participate (the only requirement involved).

The results were really amazing! While we had a few people that didn't respond or send anything, we had a majority of people send in more than the requested $10. This is a great campaign because it doesn't require an enormous amount of work for the staff at the Center. It's really about getting friends of the organization to do the work for the organization and, you'll see, the results are amazing! Expect to raise between $6,000 to $12,000 with 100 people sending 10 letters.

## Ten for Ten Campaign Letter

## Albemarle Crisis Pregnancy Center
## Ten for Ten Campaign

Dear Friend of the CPC,

Thank you so much for your willingness to participate in our Ten for Ten Campaign this year. Our goal is to have 100 friends solicit 10 of their friends for donations of $10.00, resulting in a $10,000 fundraising campaign for the CPC.

We know that in these economic times it's difficult to give even to those organizations that you hold dearest to your heart. Our ministry is so thankful for your ongoing support over the years, prayerfully, financially and physically. This campaign is a simple one that can result in a great blessing for our ministry.

This year we have seen many changes at the Center, with staff retirements and clients increasing! We are excited about the new people on board and believe that they will be true assets to our efforts to defend life and family here in northeastern North Carolina. We have much to do and believe that God will continue to supply all of our needs, as He has for the past 20 years!

Again, thank you for helping us in this endeavor. Enclosed you will find all the materials needed for your part in our campaign, along with instructions. Please feel free to contact Dee or Terry at the Center if you have any questions.

Blessings,

Dee Spruce

Executive Director

## Ten for Ten Campaign
## Donor Solicitation Letter

## Albemarle Crisis Pregnancy Center
## Ten for Ten Campaign

Dear _____,

The Albemarle Crisis Pregnancy Center is a non-profit organization that has been providing services to women and families facing crisis pregnancy situations in northeastern North Carolina since 1988. The CPC's services are provided at no cost to clients and are confidential. Services include: free pregnancy test, peer counseling, material assistance, abstinence education, parent education, and post abortion counseling.

The CPC is funded by individuals, churches, and businesses who have a heart for the unborn and families in this community. Donations are given monthly, quarterly, and through fundraising events held by the Center each year.

During the month of August, the CPC is holding its first ever *Ten for Ten Campaign* fundraiser. One hundred supporters of the center have agreed to solicit 10 of their family members or friends to donate $10 to help the center reach its goal of $10,000. And, that's right, you guessed it, I'm one of the one hundred participating!

So, I would like to ask that you prayerfully consider a check or cash donation in the amount of $10 or more to the Center today. Checks should be made payable to ACPC. I have enclosed a self-addressed envelope for your convenience. Once I have received donations from my ten family and friends, I will be mailing them to the Center. This Campaign is running from August 4<sup>th</sup> to August 28<sup>th</sup>, but I would like to get my donations in as soon as possible.

Thank you for helping me support a ministry that is so desperately needed in our area and is dear to my heart! If you would like further information about the Albemarle Crisis Pregnancy Center visit their website at www.albemarlecpc.org.

With Great Expectation,

P.S. All donations to the Albemarle Crisis Pregnancy Center are tax deductible!

### Ten for Ten Campaign Instructions

1. The campaign begins on August 4<sup>th</sup> and ends on August 28<sup>th</sup>.
2. Please prayerfully consider 10 friends or family members that would be willing to help you support our cause.

3. Once you have chosen your 10 people, we would suggest that you contact them by phone to let them know they will be receiving a letter from you requesting their support.

4. Enclosed in this package you will find 10 letters for you to fill out with your friend's names and your signature.

5. Please send the letters out in the envelopes provided, using your address as the return address on each envelope.

6. If you have not heard back from your friends within a week, please contact them by phone for a follow-up.

7. Once you have received donations from your 10 friends, please place all of the donations in the envelope provided and return to the CPC. (Please include your contact information in the envelope, as well.)

As always, we thank you for being a part of our ministry! Your faithfulness is a blessing to women and families in northeastern North Carolina that are served through the CPC offices in Edenton and Elizabeth City each year! Please feel free to contact Dee or Terry at the Center at xxx-xxxx if you have questions or concerns or if you are in need of more letters and envelopes!

## Ten for Ten Checklist:

1.  Three Months Prior:
___Form a committee to organize campaign

___Determine financial goal

___Choose date for campaign

___Determine list of 100 individuals to send out 10 letters

2.  Two Months Prior:
___Contact and confirm 100 participants

___Create and print info for packets: directions, letters, response envelopes, etc.

___Put packages together for mailing

3.  One Month Prior:
___Mail out packets to 100 participants

___Follow up with a phone call to confirm receipt of packets

4.  Two Weeks Prior to Campaign Closing:
___Contact participants: encourage, check to see if more letters or materials are    needed, remind them of closing date

# LOCK-UP!

Our Crisis Pregnancy Center started holding annual Lock-Ups several years ago. This event has been a great community awareness opportunity for us, as well as a great money maker! Our first Lock-Up event brought in around $25,000.

As with all fundraisers, get your committee together and determine how much you need to make and what you will be doing with those monies. Keep in mind that your jailbirds will be the ones soliciting the majority of those funds, other than underwriting, of course. Then, select a venue that will allow you to have your "jailbirds" on display! We have used our local coffee shop, our organization's parking lot (we are in a strip mall), and the local mall. Make sure your location has cell phone service or you will have to provide land lines through your phone company and that can get pricey!

The jest of this event is simple. Contact supporters of your organization to participate as "jailbirds." Our list has included local business owners, the fire chief, the sheriff, insurance agents, realtors, as well as administrators from the local school system and college. Each of our staff members and board members serve time as well! The "jailbirds" sentence is to raise $1,000 in bail money or sit in jail the day of your event until they do, that's it! Some of them will raise that money ahead of time and turn it in, some of them will wait until they are arrested to work on raising their bail, while others will sit in jail through the entire event and raise more than $1,000 in pledges. This fundraiser is really a lot of fun!

Now some people will want to turn themselves in, but if you want to really have some fun, have them arrested! Contact your local sheriff or police department and see if they will allow one of their officers to issue warrants and arrest participants for you. Let "jailbirds" know that if they don't turn themselves in by 10:00am they might risk being picked up by the law! Most will be willing to let that happen for the fun of it.

For my first lock-up I was arrested in our local pharmacy! That's right, handcuffs and all! While I thought seeing the high school principal arrested in the school library was hilarious, I didn't find my situation as amusing. And, by the way, I never plan to ride in the back of a sheriff's car with my hands locked behind my back again! I'll turn myself in first!

Two months prior to this event, send out your request for underwriting of up-front costs for the event. That will include all print material, t-shirts, food, and beverages for your inmates! Letters should be sent to local businesses and supporters of your organization that you depend on for underwriting your events.

Prepare a packet for each one of your participants. This packet should have a letter explaining what is required of them as a "jailbird," a pledge sheet, a donation envelope, and we always print a subpoena with their name on it charging them with failure to pay their $1,000 donation to our organization. This packet should be delivered three to four weeks prior to your event.

Include a four to six foot banner with your organizations name, logo, and Lock-Up on it to display at the event. Contact a local fence company and request fencing to use at your venue to keep your inmates "locked up." We have used vinyl fencing and the company we work with delivers and picks it up after the event!

Don't forget to prepare and distribute Press Releases to all of your media channels. You would be amazed at the amount of money raised by walk-ups who are just coming to see the locals "serving time!"

The day of the event you will need tables and chairs set up with phone books within your jail cell. We generally hold our event from 10am to 2pm and provide a light breakfast and pizza or subs for lunch. Set up a table for your magistrate to accept money and *book* your people as they turn themselves in or are brought in by officers. We have them change into our bright orange t-shirts and we do photos of everyone in handcuffs behind bars. It's hysterical!

For added incentive, you could solicit local businesses for gift certificates or a prize package to award to the "jailbird" who raises the most bail, or who raises their bail the fastest.

## Lock-Up Underwriting Letter

Dear Supporter,

How strange it is to even say that summer is drawing to a close and we are currently in the planning stages of our fall fundraiser? This year we will hold our Second Annual Lock-Up for Awareness in Edenton on October 10th and in Elizabeth City on October 24th.

You may remember last year's event and the great success we had in raising over $20,000 for this ministry! We had a great deal of fun with local pastors, law enforcement, and other jailbirds and look forward to issuing warrants for this year's participants. (All of which will stay in jail until they have raised their $1,000 bond ☺).

As you know, this ministry is neither state nor federally funded. We operate based on the generosity of local individuals, businesses, and churches just like you! God has always provided for the needs of our clients through your faithfulness to the Crisis Pregnancy Center.

This event, like our Banquet, is very important to us. It serves, not only as an opportunity to help us raise much needed funds for this ministry, but is also an opportunity to promote awareness in our community.

We would like to ask you to prayerfully consider a financial contribution to assist with the underwriting expenses of this year's Lock-Up. You are a true blessing to young women and families in this area and we appreciate you and your continued support!

Trusting Him,


"Ask and it will be given to you; seek and you will find; knock and the door will be opened to you." (Matthew 7:7)


## Lock-Up "Jailbird" Instructions


Let me begin by saying thank you for your willingness to be **Locked-Up** for teens and families in northeastern North Carolina. This event is about raising awareness of our organization and raising funds to allow us to continue to provide services to youth and families here in northeastern North Carolina.

1. As a jailbird, you are receiving a subpoena to present a $1,000 donation to the magistrate on Friday, October 26th at 10:00am. The magistrate will be available at our jail located in Acoustic Coffee, in downtown Edenton.

2. If raised prior to your appearance date, your $1,000 donation will serve as your "get out of jail free card." If not raised prior to your appearance date, a warrant will be issued for your arrest.

3. Once your warrant is issued, you will be arrested and placed in jail at Acoustic Coffee. You will be released when you have successfully presented your $1,000 bail to the magistrate.

4. While in jail you will be permitted to use your cell phone to call on those who care about you to bring in your bail money for your release. Checks should be made payable to the ACPC. Visa/MasterCard will also be accepted.

Please remember this is a fundraising and awareness event. We want you to have fun and to expect surprises along the way! If you have questions or need any information please feel free to call the office @ xxx-xxxx anytime.

With Great Anticipation!

**Lock-Up Bail Money Form**

# Get Me Out of Jail Please!
ACPC Lock-Up

**My Bail Is:$** _____

**Jailbird's Name:** _____

**Address:** _____

**City:** _____

**State/Zip** _____ **Phone** _____

All monies must be turned into the Magistrate at the Edenton Coffee House, 302 S. Broad St., in Edenton on October 23rd between 10:00am and 2:00pm or at Southgate Mall in Elizabeth City on November 6th between 10:00am and 2:00pm. Checks should be made payable to ACPC. Debit/Credit cards also accepted. Payments should be placed in Bail Money envelope.

Please PRINT Information:

Name _____

Address _____

City _____

State/Zip_____/_____Phone _____

[ ]Check                [ ]Debit/CC                [ ]Cash

Amount $_____

Credit Card Info:

Name _____

Card #_____ EXP _____/_____

Name _____

Address _____

City _____

State/Zip_____/_____Phone _____

[ ]Check                [ ]Debit/CC                [ ]Cash

Amount $_____

Credit Card Info:

Name

Card #_____ EXP _____/_____
z

Name _____

Address _____

City _____

State/Zip_____/_____Phone _____

[ ]Check                [ ]Debit/CC                [ ]Cash

Amount $_____

Credit Card Info:

Name

Card #_____ EXP _____/_____

**Total $_____(This Side)**

Please PRINT Information:

Name _____
Address _____
City _____
State/Zip_____/_____Phone _____
[ ]Check                    [ ]Debit/CC                    [ ]Cash
Amount $_____
Credit Card Info:
Name _____
Card #_____ EXP _____/_____

Name _____
Address _____
City _____
State/Zip_____/_____Phone _____
[ ]Check                    [ ]Debit/CC                    [ ]Cash
Amount $_____
Credit Card Info:
Name
Card #_____ EXP _____/_____

Name _____
Address _____
City _____
State/Zip_____/_____Phone _____
[ ]Check                    [ ]Debit/CC                    [ ]Cash
Amount $_____
Credit Card Info:
Name
Card #_____ EXP _____/_____

**Total $_____(This Side)**

TOTAL from THIS SIDE          $_____
+ TOTAL from FRONT            $_____
= TOTAL COLLECTED             $_____

## Lock-Up Bail Pledge Letter

*Albemarle Crisis Pregnancy Center*
*123 Main Street*
*Elizabeth City, NC 27909*
*xxx-xxx-xxxx*

October 30, 2007

Dear Friend of the CPC,

Thank you so much for your one-time pledge of $_____in bail money for the Albemarle Crisis Pregnancy Center Lock-Up for Awareness on Friday, October 26 at Acoustic Coffee. Enclosed you will find a self-addressed envelope for your convenience. Please include your "jailbird's" name on your memo when sending your check.

You may have been told how vital this event was to our financial stability through the rest of this year. Because of the generosity and commitment of everyone involved we have raised in gifts and pledges over $12,700! These monies will help us continue our ministry to youth and families in northeastern North Carolina!

Thank you for your faithfulness to our jailbirds☺ and the Albemarle Crisis Pregnancy Center!

Blessings,

Dee Spruce,

Executive Director

## Lock-Up Checklist:

1.  Three Months Prior:
___Form a committee to organize campaign

___Determine financial goal

___Choose time-frame for campaign

___Determine list of potential jailbirds

___Determine your venue and book

2.  Two Months Prior:
___Contact potential jailbirds for commitments

___Create letter and instructions for participants

___Create pledge forms

___Create public service announcements

___Order event banner

3.  One Month Prior:
___Mail packets to jailbirds

___Collect phone books

___Order t-shirts

___Solicit local businesses for prizes

___Contact local law enforcement for potential "arresting officer"

___Secure a pair of handcuffs

___Contact a fence company for fencing to cage your jailbirds

4. Two Weeks Prior:

___Contact participants to confirm needed "arrests" or if turning themselves in

___Purchase items needed to do photos of participants

___Contact venue to arrange time for set up and break down of event

___Distribute public service announcements to all available media outlets

5. One Week Prior:

___Gather and pack items needed for the event

___Confirm arresting officer

___Confirm magistrate

___Confirm photographer

___Contact local newspaper for coverage

# BINGO "FUN-RAISER"

## Bull Hockey Bingo

Yes, you read right, I said "Bull Hockey Bingo!" This is a fundraiser I held several years ago for our local 4H Group while serving as their Fundraising Coordinator. It was actually my husband's idea after he heard about a Cow Pie Bingo from someone at work. Yes honey, I'm giving you credit! So, I did some research and Bull Hockey Bingo was born. This is a great fundraiser for 4 H'ers, school FFA groups, Scouts, or any other group that is tied to the outdoors. In the next several pages you will find all the documentation you need to hold a Bull Hockey Bingo. But, of course, before you get started, you may want to know exactly what we're talking about.

Bull Hockey Bingo is very similar to regular Bingo, aside from the fact that you don't get bingo cards, bingo blotters and you don't sit at the local Foreign Legion or

Ruritan Club building to play it! BHB is played in a field that has been marked with chalk line to look like a giant bingo board. Blocks are numbered and tickets are sold for each block. When everyone is ready, a very "full" bull is set loose on the field and, you guessed it, go Hockey! The square that receives most of the bull's business wins a prize!

Now this may sound unpleasant, but, in all honesty, the folks in my area absolutely love it! It can certainly be adapted; you could use cows, pigs or even dogs for a scaled down version. Fundraising events aren't always the favorite place for men to go, but I have to tell you, the men were all over this one. (An incredibly important tip: an extra morning feeding and a dose of pepto bismol gets things going!)

One of the main issues to consider for this event is the venue. Our group used a local bull pen, which was ideal for us because we had all the amenities already in place: stadium seats, PA system, bulls on sight, restrooms, great parking, and they already carried insurance so it was really a no-brainer. The owner even agreed to provide two volunteers to handle the bulls at the event.

Underwriting requests for sponsorship of this event were very well received. Plan to send letters to local, state, and national vendors that provide products or services relevant to the livestock, rodeo, or farm industries. Make sure to send your letter, follow up with a phone call or email and, for goodness sakes, go into the local businesses and "Ask!"

## Bull Hockey Bingo Public Service Announcement

Galloping for the Gold, Edenton 4H Group

Galloping for the Gold 4H will hold their first annual Bull Hockey Bingo and BBQ plate luncheon Saturday, March 7 from 11am to 2pm at Top Notch Bull Pens on Rocky Hock Road. Eat there and watch the Bingo games or take out! BBQ plates are $7, provided by Nixon's Family Restaurant. Live remote broadcast from Dixie 105.7.

Bull Hockey Bingo Games will be played at noon, 1, and 2pm. $5 per square for spot on a 100 square bingo board, if the bull "Hockey's" on your square you win a $100 cash prize! One prize awarded per game. T-shirts will be on sale to commemorate the event.

Proceeds will allow the 4H'ers to participate in training and camp activities this summer.

"Bull Hockey Bingo," it's not just a game….It's a 4H adventure!"

For tickets or information call xxx-xxx-xxxx.

## Bull Hockey Bingo Flyer

### Galloping for the Gold
### 4-H Presents:

# Our First Annual Bull Hockey Bingo and BBQ Luncheon!

Come out and enjoy some real fun at the First Annual Bull Hockey Bingo. Just buy tickets for one of three games of 100 square bingo! Grab a BBQ plate, enjoy some tunes and great giveaways from the Dixie 105.7 Live Remote and wait for the bull to hockey on your square! One winner per game. $100 cash prize on each of three games. This event will benefit the Galloping for the Gold 4H Group of Edenton. See ya there!

Saturday March 29th
11 am to 2pm
Top Notch Bull Pens
Rocky Hock Road
For tickets or information call
Dee Spruce at xxx-xxxx

**Bull Hockey Bingo
Sample Ticket**

*Galloping for the Gold 4-H*

Barbecue Fundraiser

When: Saturday, March 29th

Where: Top Notch Bullpen

Time: 11:00am to 2:00pm

Ticket cost is $7.00

Nixon Family Restaurant Catering

(Come out and pick up your plate and join us for Bull Hockey Bingo!)

## Bull Hockey Bingo Galloping for the Gold 4-H Overview

Location: Top Notch Bull Pens

Time: 11:00am to 2:00pm

Fundraising Goal: $2500 to $3000

Projected Income:

Underwriting: $1000

T-Shirt Sales: $400 (40 shirts at $10.00 per shirt)

BBQ Plate Sales: $2275 (325 plates at $7.00 per plate)

Bingo Squares: $2000 (200 squares at $10.00 per square)

Total Projected Income: $5675

Projected Expenses:

T-Shirts: 300 plus tax (50 shirts)

BBQ Plates: $1218.75 (325 plates at $3.75 per plate)

Advertising: $300 (radio station remote)

Printing of Bingo Tickets: $40

Spectators Insurance: $150

Payout on Bingo Games: $400

Total Projected Expenses: $2108.75

Income less expenses: $3566.25

This event will be something new and completely different from your average fundraiser! With that in mind, we should be able to do this successfully. Everyone is going to have to pull their own weight for this to work! Tickets will be available for the BBQ plates next week and for the Bingo the following week.

## Bull Hockey Bingo Checklist:

1.  Three Months Prior:
    ___Form committee

    ___Choose date and time of event

    ___Secure venue

    ___Create budget

    ___Choose logo for print materials and t-shirts

    ___Write and distribute underwriting letters for sponsorship of event

    ___If livestock is not available at your venue, contact local farmers to arrange for   the animals to be transported and used for the event

2.  Two Months Prior:
    ___Have tickets printed

    ___Distribute tickets to committee members for sale

    ___Write Public Service Announcements (Include sponsor info)

    ___Order shirts and any signage requested by sponsors

    ___Obtain event insurance

    ___Design and print posters and flyers

Dee Spruce

___Secure emcee and three judges

___Arrange for PA system and operator

___Secure vendor to provide refreshments

3. One Month Prior:
___Push ticket sales

___Put out posters

___Contact local high school or recreational department for chalk line machine

___Line up team of volunteers to help with event

___Make sure all underwriting is completed

4. Two Weeks Prior:
___Distribute flyers

___Send PSA's to all local radio stations and newspapers

___Follow up on insurance

___Secure tables, tents or any necessary seating for event

5. One Week Prior:
___Pick up t-shirts

___Follow-up with all participants and provide specific instructions for their role

___Create poster-sized bingo boards

___Go to venue and create a map of set-up for event

6. Day Before Event:

___Final follow-up with all participants: provide written timeline, map of set-up   and t-shirt

___Contact venue to ensure time of access for set up

___Meet with chalk line artist to map out bingo board (weather permitting)

7. Day of Event:

___Arrive at least half an hour before other participants to get everything   together and ready for a successful event!

___Play Bingo!

# WALK-A-THONS

Our ministry held Walks for Life until a few years ago because it seemed that every non-profit in our area was doing the same! Prior to that issue we had very successful walk-a-thon events. This is yet another way to get your supporters to do the fundraising for you!

As with any event, choose your date and walk site. The site should be one that will allow your group to participate in a two mile walk route. Perhaps a downtown park or historic district is available in your area; or you could choose the track or gymnasium of a local high school or college. This event is not only a fundraiser, but a community awareness opportunity. So, keep that in mind when choosing your location. Also, make sure there are restroom facilities available at your site.

If you choose a park or downtown area, you will need to contact your town's law enforcement office and Department of Parks and Recreation to schedule the event and to obtain the necessary permits. We also request a police escort to assist with the walk route and closing off of any streets that may be needed. You will need to decide if you want to do a "rain date" or make this a rain or shine event and plan accordingly. Remember to work with your law enforcement to map out the walk route so that you can include that in your print materials for walkers.

Keep in mind that this is a walk and not a "march." All participants need to understand that it is a peaceful event that will serve to promote your ministry and not a picketing opportunity of any sort! Some of our groups have elected to carry banners identifying their group or church, and that is permissible; however, do not include any signage or statements that would draw offense.

Upon selecting your time and date, begin thinking about a theme for your event, then set a budget of anticipated costs and income. If you set a goal of 100 walkers raising $250 each, you can expect $25,000 in income, along with any underwriting of the up-front costs. That, of course, should be solicited from businesses and friends of your organization that you can count on for support.

With your goals in mind, form a Walk Committee. This Committee should work on designing all print materials and t-shirts for your event, as well as ordering an eight foot registration and start banner. They should also commit to contacting individuals or groups that may be willing to walk in your walk-a-thon. Those contacts should be made two months prior to your event. Our organization uses recruiters from our supporting churches and requests that they organize groups of ten walkers for the event. Also, form a committee to work on set-up and break-down the day of the event.

We have found that the best way to get our recruiters pumped up about the event is to host a Walk Recruiters Brunch. This event allows you to share information about your organization, explain the role of the recruiter, the goal of the walk and distribute an information packet to each with all the materials needed to promote the event and build their team.

Walk Recruiter Packets should include a thank you letter for their commitment, information about your organization, and the goal of the event. Each recruiter should be given a t-shirt, a map of the walk route, flyers and posters for their church, and walk pledge forms and donation envelopes for the ten on their team. The brunch should be held approximately six weeks before the event.

To promote your goal of $150 or $250 raised by each walker, offer a free t-shirt to everyone who reaches that level in pledges. I would also solicit local businesses and put together prize packages for the youth walker who raises the most money, as well as the adult walker who raises the most money. These prize packages have included: t-shirts, restaurant gift cards, gift cards from our local Christian book stores, movie tickets, and we once even had a weekend trip to give away donated by a local travel agency. We have also arranged for pizza parties for the group that raises the most money.

When doing your pledge sheets be sure to request name, address, and contact number on all donations. If you accept credit cards, remember to request the necessary information for that, as well. Make sure to provide a box to check if they want to be billed or if the pledge is paid. Our policy is that we bill for pledges over $10.00, but request that walkers collect anything under that amount. We also note that donation receipts are available upon request. That saves a great deal in mailing costs for donations of small amounts.

Have committee members contact recruiters on a weekly basis to assess how they are doing and see if they need more pledge forms or information. This will also serve as a motivation to them along the way!

Write and distribute Public Service Announcements about your event to all media channels at least two weeks prior to your event. Be sure to mention any sponsors in your announcements who have requested this service. Don't forget your website, twitter, and facebook! It would also be helpful if you develop a registration form and provide a downloadable pledge form on your website (make those available online one month prior to the event).

Make sure to secure any sound equipment or staging you may need at least one month prior to the event. You may even choose to tie into a local radio station and request a live remote. This may come at a cost to your organization, but you can solicit that in your underwriting.

One month prior to the event, you will need to set up a team for registration. These individuals will be available on-site to register any walk up participants and collect donations from individuals and teams for a one hour period prior to the event. This should be announced as "registration time" on all print materials. A team of eight to ten should be sufficient to handle between 200 and 400 walkers.

The registration area should be set up in a closed square of eight foot tables. Chairs should be made available on the inside of the square for your registration team. Each person handling registration should have a red pen, black pen, calculator, stapler, raffle tickets, extra pledge forms and donation envelopes on hand. Also, purchase an accordion binder for filing pledge forms and donation envelopes.

Your Registration Team should be selected and provided with brief instructions prior to the event on how to handle donations and pledge sheets. These basic instructions are there to help with any confusion that might occur with pledge sheets and monies turned in and, yes, at times, there is confusion! Upon accepting a pledge form and donation envelope:

1. Add the total pledges on the form and write that amount in the upper right hand corner in red ink.
2. Place a slash mark from the upper left hand corner to the lower right hand corner of each pledge (we put boxes on our pledge forms that are marked as turned in). Then, add the money provided in the envelope and write that amount on the envelope in black ink with your initials.
3. On the pledge envelope, under the total pledges written in red, take your black ink pen and write the amount of donations turned in with your initials.
4. Staple the pledge form to the donation envelope and place it in the accordion file.
5. Give walkers who have met the requested goal a t-shirt with a ticket to take to your t-shirt table. (We use raffle tickets or stickers).

You will also need to set up a table at the event for t-shirts. This table should accept the tickets or stickers you give at registration in exchange for t-shirts for participants who qualify. You may also sell t-shirts as an extra source of income at the event.

I would also suggest a booth that provides information on your organization and an opportunity for people to sign up for your mailing or e-mail list. You might also put together packets for any potential volunteer or board applicants. This booth should be manned by a staff, board member, or volunteer that is capable of answering questions about your organization.

A booth should also be set up to provide refreshments for your walkers. Contact local beverage distributors for donations of water, Gatorade, or sodas. Have them available after the walk at no charge to your participants. Over the years we have also contacted women's groups at churches and local merchants to provide fruit or baked goods to walkers.

You might consider contacting a group or restaurant to provide lunch depending on what time you hold your walk. Make prior arrangements to promote the group or restaurant if they will be selling food as a vendor. Anyone making a profit by selling food items at your event should agree to donate a portion of their proceeds to your organization.

Choose an emcee for your walk site. If you go with a live remote from a local radio station, perhaps their DJ would assist as your emcee. This person should welcome everyone, keep your program flowing (if you decide to have one), and count down your walk start. They should also explain the walk route and any communication from law enforcement that is helping with your event. We have used local television personalities, pastors, as well as local government officials to serve as emcees.

To make sure things flow smoothly with our walk, we provide walkie-talkie radios to a designated person in the front and back of our walker's during the walk, along with radios for law enforcement and the Agency Director. By doing this, we know when to expect our group back and can track their pace and progress. Walkie-talkies can be borrowed from your local Radio Shack with a simple letter to the Store Manager (or at least, that has been the case for us). If not, I am sure you can track some down through your community of contacts!

Another good idea, for counting purposes, is to get two hand held clickers and give them to two people who agree to stand on each side of your start banner. Let them use those to count the number of walkers you have participating.

A brief program is a great idea for your event, especially during your registration time. You may choose to contact a local school or church that might provide skits or musical entertainment.

During the walk, our Board Treasurer and Office Manager or Bookkeeper add all the pledge forms so that we can announce our totals during our closing statements at the event.

After your event, follow-up with all sponsors, vendors, and each recruiter to provide them with totals on their teams' accomplishments. Be sure to send thank you notes, as well, which will assure everyone's willingness to participate next year!

## Walk-a-thon Underwriting Letter

July 26, 2001

"For we walk by faith, not by sight." (2 Corinthians 5:7)

Dear Friend of the CPC,

Our annual Walk for Life Fundraiser is Saturday, September 29th. As you know, the walk and banquet are our two major fundraisers for the year. The funds brought in at each of these events have allowed us to assist over 6,000 women who were dealing with crisis pregnancy situations since 1988. I have enclosed some information for you showing the services we have provided for these women.

As this ministry continues to grow, so does the need for further support, prayerful, physical, and financial. In order to be able to use all of the gifts raised through these fundraising events for direct ministry support, we attempt to get the underwriting costs of the events up-front. Each year we call upon our supporters to assist as they feel led with these costs.

We greatly appreciate your support of the CPC and ask that you prayerfully consider a one-time gift to assist us with the underwriting costs of the Walk for Life. This year we have a financial need (from the Walk) of over $25,000 in order to meet budget. With your help, we will be able to cover all expenses and meet or BEAT our goal!

As always, our prayers are for God's richest blessings on you and yours!

For Life!

Dee Spruce

Executive Director

## Walk-a-thon Recruiter Letter

Dear Walk Recruiter,

I cannot begin to tell you how excited we are that you have committed to be your church's contact for this year's Walk for Life. If, at anytime, you have questions or concerns about the walk, please feel free to contact a member of our staff in the Elizabeth City office.

We have enclosed in this packet everything you will need to promote this event to your congregation. This year's walk goal is $25,000 and we have to meet our goal to keep the Center doors open! This may seem like a great deal of money, but raising it should not be an issue if each of our churches will commit to raising $1,000 as a team.

Please remember, we will be awarding a weekend get-away to the Pastor and his wife of the congregation raising the most money, as well as a private pizza party at the Chowan Teen Center for the Youth Group raising the most funds. T-shirts are given to any walker who raises $150 or more. (One t-shirt per walker).

Share this information as soon as possible and begin building our team of walkers! We want to fill the park and streets of Elizabeth City this year and to do that we need YOU!

Walking for Life,

Dee Spruce

Executive Director

## Walk-a-thon Walk for Life Recruiter Instructions

1.  PROMOTIONS
    *   Bulletin Inserts: please make copies of the inserts in your packet and ask for permission to pass them out at Service or to put them directly in your bulletins.
    *   Contact Information: don't forget to fill out your contact information on the bottom, before making copies. Also, remember to be available at the door on the day you pass them out to recruit walkers and gather pledges from those who are unable to walk.
    *   Walk Information Table: ask your Pastor

first, then choose a day to wear your walk
shirt and set up an information table at the
back of the church or in the vestibule. Man
the table before and after Service so that
you can recruit walkers and take pledges.
Remember, those who can't walk can still
pledge!

- T-Shirt: your t-shirt is an excellent tool for
advertising the event. Please wear it as often
as you can!

2. PLEDGE FORMS

- Pledge Collection: please collect pledge
money prior to the Walk to turn in at
registration. Any pledges of $10 or more
can be billed if needed. Please keep in mind,
this does add extra expense for the ministry.
Pledges of less than $10 must be collected
prior to the walk. It is also suggested that
in the first space on your form, you list an
individual who has pledged $20 or more.
Most sponsors will give a pledge amount
that is comparable to others on your form.

- Sponsor Letter: the out-of-town sponsor
letter is a great tool! Each of your walkers
should be given at least five of these letters
to fill out and mail to friends and family.
Please have walkers include any out-of-town
sponsors on their forms. Also, make sure the
walker information is filled out completely

on the sponsor letters so that proper credit can be given.

3. DAY OF WALK
   - Registration: registration will begin promptly at 9:00am. Everyone must register prior to the Walk. The walk begins at 10:00am.
   - Walk: the walk is approximately two miles. We have an established route and we will all walk together. Please remember this is a fundraising and community awareness event. This is not a DEMONSTRATION! Signs, banners, etc. will not be permitted. Remember, this event doesn't end with the walk alone. We will meet after the walk where you can enjoy food, fellowship, face painting, informational booths, and lots of fun!

### Walk-a-thon Checklist:

1. Three Months Prior:
___Form a committee to organize campaign

___Determine financial goal

___Choose date and venue

___Determine list of church or civic groups to serve as recruiters

___Determine your walk route and starting area

___If needed, contact Parks and Rec Department for any booking details

___Contact local law enforcement to check on parade/walk-a-thon permits

___Determine date for recruiter's brunch and chose venue and caterer

2.  Two Months Prior:
___Send underwriting letters

___Choose theme for walk

___Contact recruiters for commitments to participate

___Create letter and instructions for recruiters

___Create pledge forms and flyers

___Create public service announcements

___Order t-shirts

___Create and distribute invitations for Recruiter's Brunch

___Create agenda/program for brunch

3.  One Month Prior:
___Put together packets for recruiters

___Hold brunch

___Put together registration team

___Solicit local businesses for prizes

___Secure sound system and emcee for event

___Contact local musicians to perform prior to and immediately following event

___Arrange for face painting or other booths at registration area (optional)

___Solicit local businesses for water, Gatorade, and snacks to distribute at event

___Organize team for set up, break down, and distribute refreshments

___Follow up with recruiters on a weekly basis for any needed assistance

(more forms and encouragement)

4. Two Weeks Prior:

___Contact emcee, musicians, and registration team to confirm

___Confirm all permits are in place

___Contact venue to arrange time for set up and break down of event

___Distribute public service announcements to all available media outlets

___Hold training for registration team

5. One Week Prior:

___Gather and pack items needed for the event

___Contact local newspaper for coverage

___Secure walkie-talkies and clickers for counting participants

___Secure photographer

___Contact local newspaper for coverage

# GOLF TOURNAMENTS

Seems only fitting that I would be writing this section on Golf Tournaments in the midst of planning my CPC's 3rd Annual Golf Classic! I am new to these events, however; our tournament last year received many comments to being one of the "best" our golfers had ever attended! With that said, I believe I can assist those of you who are new to these events, and may be able to provide some thoughts to you experts as well! I must admit though that last year I went in blindly with the help of our Board Chairperson who had organized several in the past! So, I will personally lend credit here to her; thank you Shelley Layden.

As usual, form a committee! Organize this committee at least three months in advance. Choose your date and location for the event. We use our local Golf and Country Club. Make sure you choose carefully. We use the one that offers us the best deal, as you should also. By a deal, I mean a discount on cart and green fees for our players, a good price on lunch, and not a great demand on what we have to purchase from their pro shop. And, they purchase our insurance (we pay, of course, but they do all the paperwork) for the "Million Dollar Hole in One" or "Car Give-Away" and agree to oversee the tournament.

Now, if you're looking for advice on all the elements of the game itself…you may be in trouble here! However, if you want to learn how to go after your teams, sponsors, and set up the tournament, then this is the chapter for you! I gladly passed on the running of the tourney the day of the event. You need to find a pro for that one! But I learned a lot and we pulled off a great tournament!

Once you have the date and venue, your committee should work with the Country Club to determine your menu. Our tournaments are held in the morning, so we provide a light continental breakfast and then a prime rib lunch following. Once that is determined, they can get to work organizing your print materials. This should include a three-fold flyer with a section that can be removed and mailed into the Center with sponsorship and team registration information of participants. Create posters to be distributed and posted in local businesses, as well as golf courses. Amazingly, we had no trouble with one course promoting another courses event; it seems that golfers just love to golf!

Publicity is a big deal for this event! We obtain a list of all the golfers who have played at the course in tournaments over the last year. As soon as our date is chosen, we mail them a save-the-date postcard. Then, approximately one month prior to the tournament, we mail the registration and sponsorship flyers to all of those players. Get your Public Service Announcements out to all media outlets. Include information on the internet and make downloadable registration forms available on your website.

The biggest part of putting this monster on is truly getting your sponsorships done! Have your committee come up with a large list of local businesses that can be called upon for different levels of sponsorships or donations; we determine sponsorship levels. For example, a Gold or Title Sponsor might be $2,500 and includes: a four man team, a six to eight foot banner signage at registration, a mention in all print materials and advertising, their logo on hats or shirts as a main sponsor, and the ability to place marketing materials on tables or in gift bags. A Silver Sponsor may include: a signage on all tables as sponsor of prime rib luncheon, a mention in print materials, as well as the ability to place marketing materials on tables or in gift bags. The beauty of it is the fact that you can play with what you are willing to offer the individual sponsors in exchange for their donation. By the way, we promote four man teams at $100 a player or single players can register and get placed on a team.

We also offer tee or hole sponsorships. For $150 businesses get a signage at one of the holes on the course. We have logos printed on two and a half foot, round, giant golf balls placed on tees. We had a lot of comments on those signs and, in fact, several other tournaments have used that idea! Our goal is at least one sponsor for every hole. You may also solicit a business to sponsor the "Million Dollar Hole" or the chance to "Win a Car" for the cost of the insurance. A car dealership would obviously be a good choice for that promotion and they could even bring a car out to the course the day of the event!

With a group working on soliciting the sponsorships, you then need a group who will focus on prizes, giveaways, and snacks. Our golf course allows us to provide a snack cart free of charge to our teams. We solicit donations from local businesses of beverages and food items like nabs (sorry, "southern term") or peanut butter crackers, peanuts, popcorn, pretzels, etc.

We organize gift bags for each player and present them at registration. Bags have been donated by one of our local cell phone dealers and one of our local community colleges. These gift bags are filled with donated items like tees, drink huggies (you know, the things that insulate your beverage), towels, golf balls, pens, magnets, cups, pads, and key chains from local businesses. We have also solicited larger distributors of golf supplies for items for these bags. Simply contact their Corporate Office; they often merely require a written request. This, of course, should be done six to eight weeks prior to your event to allot time to receive these gifts.

We also "ask" local businesses for gift certificates and items to give away in our raffle. Each player that registers is given a raffle ticket and we do our best to have a giveaway for everyone present. Our giveaways were said to be the best last year! We had golf clubs, shirts, golf bags, chairs, restaurant gift certificates, golf paintings; you name it, we had it! We also determine what prizes to award our First and Second Place teams. To help our golf course, we usually do a $100 gift card to the pro shop for each member of the First Place team and a $50 gift card for each member of the Second Place team.

At the event, during registration, we offer the chance to purchase score assists, mulligans, and red tees. The Pro from the golf club gives the instructions and starts the tournament. He also provides us with our winners, so once they are on the course playing, it's all done except cruising in the snack cart and taking pictures! Then, we all enjoy lunch, award our prizes, and do our raffle and call it a day!

## Golf Tournaments Sponsor Letter

Dear Friend,

We are all fortunate enough to be able to worship in the place of our choice. We have food at hand and access to doctors and medicines of any variety. We have shelter, clothes, vehicles, and a number of items I could go on to list. Last, but not least, we have an opportunity, an opportunity to help others less fortunate than ourselves.

The Albemarle Crisis Pregnancy Center has been dedicated to reaching out to women and families in northeastern North Carolina for over 20 years. We have been fortunate enough to provide assistance to thousands who are dealing with crisis pregnancy situations. We have been able to reach out to teens in our public schools, youth groups, local colleges and juvenile detention centers spreading the abstinence message. We have provided choices to women who felt that the only choice was abortion. We have provided support to new mothers and babies through our Creative Parenting Program. And we have shared the grace, mercy, and forgiveness of Jesus Christ to women seeking healing through our post-abortion bible study program, PACE (Post Abortion Counseling Education). We are continuing our efforts and are constantly searching for new and exciting ways to reach out to those in need.

We will be holding our First Annual Golf Classic on Thursday, June 19th at the Chowan Golf and Country Club in Edenton, North Carolina. This tournament will allow us to raise the needed funds to help us continue our ministry to women and families here in northeastern North Carolina. We would appreciate your help with a donation towards this event. There are a number of ways to help, donations in the form of cash, prizes, food, gift bags, as well as participation in the tournament itself would be greatly appreciated. All proceeds will benefit the programs of the Albemarle Crisis Pregnancy Center.

Please see the enclosed brochure for information on how you can assist with this exciting event! Your donations to the Golf Classic are tax deductible. Event sponsors will be included in all advertising and spotlighted in our monthly newsletter.

Thank you for your time and consideration. Please feel free to contact the Center with any questions at xxx-xxxx.

With Great Expectation!

## Golf Tournaments Public Service Announcement

Albemarle Crisis Pregnancy Center Holds it's Second Annual Golf Classic

The Albemarle Crisis Pregnancy Centers of Elizabeth City and Edenton will hold their 2nd Annual Golf Classic on Friday, May 15th at the Chowan Golf and Country Club. Shotgun Start at 8:30am with great prizes and giveaways! A prime rib lunch will be served after the tournament. Prizes and Giveaways include: clubs, golf store gift cards, balls, gift items and certificates from area merchants! On course snacks and beverages provided, as well!

Proceeds from this tournament will allow the centers to continue providing services to women and families facing crisis pregnancies in northeastern North Carolina. If you are interested in organizing a team for the tournament or donating to this event please call the center @ xxx.xxxx or Dee Spruce @ xxx.xxxx.

## Golf Tournament Registration Form

Albemarle Crisis Pregnancy Center presents the Golf Classic golfers look forward to year after year!

Friday, May 21st 9:00 a.m. Shotgun start!
The Sound Golf Links, Albemarle Plantation, Herford, NC

Register Today! Limited to 88 Players

| Sign Up For | Price: |
|---|---|
| ___ Title Sponsorship | 2,500.00 |

(Includes one foursome)

| | |
|---|---|
| ___ Gold Sponsor | 1,500.00 |
| Gold Sponsor Foursome | |
| 375.00 | |
| Team Captain ......................... | |
| ___ Silver Sponsor | |
| 750.00 | |
| ___ Silver Sponsor Foursome | |
| 375.00 | |
| Team Captain ......................... | |
| ___ Tee Sponsor | |
| 150.00 | |
| ___ Single Player | |
| 100.00 | |
| ___ Four Person Team | |
| 400.00 | |
| Team Captain ......................... | |

4-Player Best Ball

Mulligans

& Other Score Saving Assists

Practice Range Balls

Steak Lunch

Prize Awards

On-Course Snacks &

Beverages

**Longest Drive**

**& Closest to**

**The Pin Contest**

**Please note: The Sound Golf**

**Links is a soft spike facility.**

**Dress code strictly enforced:**

**no jeans and shirt must have a**

**collar.**

Send entry form and

sponsorship payable to:

ACPC

123 Main Street

Elizabeth City, NC

27909

Call for information:

XXX.XXX.XXXX

Encouraging Teens
Empowering Women
Enhancing Families

___ I do not golf but would like to volunteer at the event.

Name: ...................................

Address: ...................................

...................................

Email: ...................................

Phone: ...................................

## Golf Tournament Checklist:

1. Three Months Prior:
___Form a committee to organize tournament

___Determine financial goal

___Choose date

___Contact local golf course and book your tournament

___Gather lists of addresses from local country clubs of potential players

___Determine lists of potential underwriters and large sponsors

___Create post-card for event and mail to list of potential players

2. Two Months Prior:
___Send underwriting letters

___Contact and secure contract for catered luncheon

___Create registration form and brochure

___Contact local businesses for prizes, giveaways, and title sponsorships

___Create flyers and distribute

___Create public service announcements

___Solicit for hole sponsorships

3. One Month Prior:
___Order signage for hole sponsors

___Put together prize packages and giveaway bags

___Put together registration team

___Solicit local businesses for on-course beverage and snack donations

___Secure sound system and emcee for event

4. Two Weeks Prior:
___Contact emcee and registration team to confirm

___Confirm number of registered players with golf course

___Arrange time for set up and break down of event

___Distribute public service announcements to all available media outlets

___Hold training for registration team

5. One Week Prior:
___Pick up donated on-course refreshments

___Arrange for coolers for snack carts

___Contact local newspaper for coverage

___Secure photographer

## The Importance of Follow-Up in Fundraising!

I cannot begin to explain to you the importance of follow-up after any fundraising event. This is your opportunity to celebrate the success of what you have accomplished, while giving credit to all of those who made it possible. Your follow-up methods should be included in your fundraising event plan.

Follow-up phone calls, thank-you notes, and letters are an excellent opportunity for you to ensure that new donors and supporters are not lost. This will also serve as a way to keep your current donors and supporters connected with your organization's events and accomplishments.

Make sure the follow-up includes specific details about your event including: date, time, number of participants, an approximate total raised, as well as your original goal. One of two things will occur as a result. If you've met and exceeded your goal, it will serve as confirmation that your organization is on track and has a community of supporters that are willing to help you rise to the next level! If you don't meet your goal, the result can serve as a catalyst for those who are involved to step things up in their support efforts, which, in turn, will help you take your organization to the next level! Win-win situations are the best!

I pray this book encourages you and guides you along the path to reaching your organization's financial goals this year and for years to come! And remember, "You won't have if you don't ask!"